A L A S K A
W I L D L I F E

A Photo Memory

Photographed by Johnny Johnson

Published by

Todd Communications

Anchorage Juneau Fairbanks Kodiak Nome Denali National Park, Alaska, U.S.A.
Whitehorse, Yukon, Canada

Published by Todd Communications
203 W. 15th Ave., Suite 102
Anchorage, Alaska 99501-5128
Phone: (907) 274-8633
Fax: (907) 276-6858
e-mail: info@toddcom.com

Editor: Flip Todd
Designer: Tina Wallace
Text & Captions: Janice Berry
Photography: Johnny Johnson

Printed in Korea by Samhwa Printing Co., Ltd.
20, 19, 18, 17, 16, 15, 14, 13, 12, 11, 10, 9, 8, 7, 6, 5, 4, 3, 2

Library of Congress Catalog Card Number 99-67500

Cover
A grizzly bear *(Ursus arctos horribilis)* carries a sockeye (red) salmon from the McNeil River State Game Sanctuary in June.

Pages 2-3
Alpenglow at sunset silhouettes a brown bear *(Ursus arctos)* exploring the shore of Naknek Lake in Katmai National Park and Preserve in September.

ALASKA
WILDLIFE

A Photo Memory

Left - A bull moose *(Alces alces)* with antlers in the velvet phase browses on dwarf birch and willow. The dark, fuzzy velvet contains blood vessels that carry nutrients to help the antlers grow. When the antlers have completed their growth cycle, the velvet begins to itch and moose rub their antlers against trees to scrape it off.

Right - Twin moose calves play while their mother watches in Denali National Park and Preserve in May. Cow moose usually bear single calves in the spring, however, the better the habitat, the more likely a moose will have twins. Females with young calves can be very aggressive in order to protect their vulnerable offspring from potential predators such as bears and wolves.

Below - Winter will soon bring an end to this cow moose's feeding spot in Wonder Lake in Denali National Park and Preserve. Moose feed on pondweed found on the bottom of many Alaska lakes. North America's highest peak, 20,320-foot Mount McKinley, and the Alaska Range fill the horizon.

A cow moose lifts her head from the bottom of Horseshoe Lake in Denali National Park in July. Moose like the succulent vegetation that grows at the bottom of Alaska lakes which provide electrolytes, magnesium and sodium, critical for body function. Moose noses have a bulging valve that can be shut to keep the water out.

Below - A large bull moose *(Alces alces)*, in prime condition to survive a harsh winter, ambles amidst autumn colors of Denali National Park and Preserve in September.

Next page - A young wolf *(Canis lupus)* watches in readiness to catch one of the red (sockeye) salmon attempting to jump Brooks Falls in Katmai National Park and Preserve. The salmon return from the ocean to spawn in the lakes upriver in July.

Above - Summer's sun warms a wolf resting in a meadow filled with tundra flowers in Denali National Park and Preserve in June. Wolves range over most of Alaska including arctic tundra, brushy areas and rain forests. They mate in February and March, giving birth to an average of five pups in May or early June.

Right - A lean gray timber wolf *(Canis lupus)* pauses at the edge of the Brooks River in Katmai National Park in Southwestern Alaska. Wolves in southern Alaska are darker and slightly smaller than those in the Arctic. They inhabit all of mainland Alaska, as well as Unimak Island in the Aleutians and major islands in Southeast Alaska except Admiralty, Baranof and Chichigof.

Next page - A gravel bar provides a good resting spot for a young red fox *(Vulpes vulva)*. Red foxes live throughout Alaska except for most areas in Prince William Sound and Southeast Alaska. They are very curious, but remain wary. These omnivorous mammals are related to dogs.

Left - A blue-phase adult arctic fox *(Alopex lagopus)* hunts for birds in July among arctic lupine *(Lupinus arcticus)* on treeless St. George Island, one of the two major Pribilof Islands in the Bering Sea. The Pribilofs are also home to 176 species of birds.

Below - Arctic fox kits huddle near their den in the Arctic National Wildlife Refuge in Northeast Alaska in July. The kits will turn white as winter approaches and then back to a darker color in the spring.

An arctic fox in its white winter coat waits patiently along the Arctic coast in November. In the spring the arctic fox's coat will turn brown to blend in with the Arctic tundra. For its size (six to ten pounds), the arctic fox has the thickest fur of any polar animal. Arctic foxes often travel great distances over the sea ice when food becomes scarce, often following polar bears to feed off the remains of leftover seals and whales.

A red-throated loon *(Gavia stellata)* swims on a small lake in July. Red-throated loons prefer smaller and shallower lakes than the four other types of loons. They nest on shores and islands, flying to larger lakes and the ocean to feed.

Right - In boldly contrasting breeding plumage, a Pacific loon *(Gavia pacifica)* floats on a tundra lake in the Arctic National Wildlife Refuge in northeast Alaska. In the winter loons fly south and turn a mottled gray.

Below - A yellow-billed loon *(Gavia adamsii)*, the largest of five loon species in Alaska, rests on its nest at 2:00 a.m. under the midnight sun in the Arctic National Wildlife Refuge.

A great horned owl *(Bubo virginianus)* stays close to its nest and chick in Denali National Park and Preserve in May. Alaska is home to nine species of owls including some of the largest and most powerful in North America, such as the great horned, snowy and great gray owl.

Right - A Lesser Canada goose *(Branta canadensis parvipes)* struts amidst dandelions near Cheney Lake in east Anchorage in June. The goose population has greatly expanded in the last decade in Anchorage thanks to the increase in grassy areas like golf courses. Grass is their principal food source. They have become so plentiful they are considered a hazard to airplanes.

Below - A pair of Lesser Canada geese leads their goslings on a July cruise through Potter Marsh in south Anchorage near Turnagain Arm.

Left - A male willow ptarmigan *(Lagopus lagopus)* in spring plumage sits atop a white spruce tree. The willow ptarmigan is Alaska's state bird, chosen by Alaskan school children in 1955, four years before Alaska became the 49th state in the United States.

Below - A willow ptarmigan in fall plumage stands in the first snow of September at Denali National Park and Preserve. The chicken-like bird turns completely white in winter and back to darker plumage in the spring. Ptarmigan are more resistant to cold weather than mammals since they have no ears or tails to dissipate heat. Their feathers provide excellent insulation and they have a high metabolic rate that generates heat.

Right - Black-billed magpies *(Pica pica)*, common throughout most of Alaska, make their presence known with loud calls. Members of the same bird family as jays and crows, they are among the smartest birds in terms of deductive thinking. They build very large domed nests made of branches in bushes and trees.

Below - A male spruce grouse *(Dendragapus canadensis)* in fall plumage rests in a white spruce tree in Denali National Park and Preserve in September. Males are recognizable by the red combs over their eyes.

Right - A tufted puffin (*Fratercula cirrhata*) in summer mating colors balances expertly on a cliff in July on St. George Island in the Pribilof Islands.

Left - A horned puffin (*Fratercula corniculata*) perches on a jagged cliff near its burrow on St. Paul Island in the Pribilof Islands. Puffins come ashore to breed and nest, spending winters in the ocean feeding.

Below - Trumpeter swans (*Cygnus buccinator*) rest on Summit Lake on the Kenai Peninsula in Southcentral Alaska during the fall migration to warmer climates in September. They are the largest members of the waterfowl family, one of three species of swans that migrate to Alaska.

Left - This pair of bald eagles *(Haliaeetus leucocephalus)* has returned to their nest on 28-mile long Adak Island in the Aleutians. Eagles on Adak Island nest on cliffs and sea stacks because there are no trees on the island. They can be very aggressive when they have chicks in their nest.

Below - A bald eagle returns to its nest on Adak Island, which is about midway down the 1,100 mile-long chain of Aleutian Islands (the world's longest small-island archipelago). The Aleutian Islands are called the birthplace of storms due to the harsh climate.

Right - A small piece of ice in College Fjord, Prince William Sound provides a rest stop for a bald eagle *(Haliaeetus leucocephalus)* in June. Alaska has the largest number of bald eagles in the world with an estimated 20,000 nesting pairs.

Below - A lone bald eagle claims a snow-covered cottonwood branch in October near Haines, a small harbor town in Southeast Alaska. The area attracts thousands of bald eagles in the winter due to a late salmon run caused by warm springs in the Chilkat River.

Next page - Bald eagles congregate along the Chilkat River near Haines in October to feast on the last major run of spawning salmon. Every fall the Alaska Chilkat Bald Eagle Preserve hosts the largest gathering in the world of bald eagles. More than 3,000 birds can be seen in trees along the river.

Left - A mature Dall sheep *(Ovis dalli)* ram stands on a mountaintop in Denali National Park and Preserve. Dall sheep are the only white, wild sheep in the world and remain white year-round.

Below - A female *(ewe)* Dall sheep climbs a hill with two lambs in Denali National Park and Preserve. Ewes give birth to only one lamb, but often baby-sit while other ewes feed.

Left - A band of Dall sheep rams *(Ovis dalli)* feeds on lower mountain slopes in Denali National Park. Fifty miles away, a clear sky reveals Mt. McKinley's snow-capped summit, the highest mountain in North America at 20, 320 feet.

Below - A Dall sheep ewe glances warily over her shoulder as she nurses her lamb. Lambs are usually born from mid-May through mid-June. Single births are the most common. Lambs have a low survival rate because of the harsh environment in the rugged terrain of central and northern Alaska.

Right - Arctic ground squirrels *(Spermophilus parryii)* are common in much of Interior Alaska. They are an important food source for birds and many predatory mammals like wolves. They hibernate in winter.

Left- A snowshoe hare *(Lepus americanus)* in its summer coat feeds on willow bark in July in Denali National Park and Preserve. These rodents turn a mottled color in the fall and spring and pure white in the winter. They mate in April with the first litter of three or four born in May. Some have up to three litters per year, with only a 36-day gestation period.

Below - The combination of waning daylight and cooler temperatures causes the snowshoe hare's fur to become completely white as camouflage against predators. Principal predators are lynx, fox, marten, hawks, owls and humans.

Right - A bull walrus may weigh several thousand pounds and though graceful at sea, is awkward when coming ashore to rest. This bull came ashore in the Walrus Islands State Game Sanctuary in July. Both male and female walrus have tusks, which can grow to a yard long.

Below - About 25 miles off Alaska's southwest coast, thousands of bull walrus *(Odobenus rosmarus)* haul out on Round Island in the Walrus Islands State Game Sanctuary to rest after several days of feeding in the Bering Sea's cold waters. Walrus have a diet made up of clams, crabs and other bottom-dwelling invertebrates.

A beaver *(Castor canadensis)* swims near its lodge and food cache on a September afternoon in Denali National Park and Preserve. A lodge typically houses two adults, four newborn kits and four yearling kits.

Above - Willow leaves are a principal food for beaver. The beaver is the largest North American rodent. Other food sources include bark and cambium, the live layer between the bark and the trunk of willow, poplar, birch and aspen, as well as herbs, ferns and grass.

Right - A beaver hauls willow branches over a dam to a food cache near its lodge in September. Beavers are dedicated dam builders, creating ponds for protection from predators such as wolves, coyotes, wolverine, lynx, bears and humans. The ponds must be made deep enough not to freeze solid during winter.

A Steller sea lion *(Eumetopias jubatus)* bellows a warning from its rocky perch in Kenai Fjords National Park in Southcentral Alaska in July. Alaska is home to about 70 percent of the world's Steller sea lion population which ranges along a North Pacific arc from Japan to California.

Above - Steller sea lions frolic near their haulout on Round Island in the Walrus Islands State Game Sanctuary. The Sanctuary consists of seven islands off Alaska's Southwest coast in Bristol Bay. Named by the German naturalist Georg Steller, on Vitus Bering's 1741 voyage of discovery to Alaska, these pinnipeds have been classified as a threatened species since 1990. Their population has plummeted for a variety of reasons including increased competition with the commercial fishing fleet for their primary food source, pollock.

Below - Harbor seals (Phoca vitulina) gather on ice chunks from nearby glaciers in College Fjord, Prince William Sound.   Of the seven species of seals in Alaska, the harbor seal is the most common, occurring in the southeast and southwestern regions and the Aleutian Islands.

A sea otter *(Enhydra lutris)* spy hops for a better look at its surroundings in Prince William Sound. Sea otters stay within a few miles of land, but rarely go ashore, even giving birth at sea. Commonly found near kelp beds, this smallest of marine mammals eats sea urchins, crabs and clams while floating on its back. They weigh up to 80 pounds and have webbed back paws for swimming while the front ones have fingers with retractable claws for prying abalone and other bivalves from the sea bed.

Above - Sockeye (red) salmon *(Onchorhynchus nerka)* fight their way over Brooks Falls in the Katmai National Park and Preserve in July to spawn in the waters where they were born. Sockeye (a corruption of sukkai, a southern British Columbia Indian name) are commonly called red salmon because of their deep red flesh and bright red bodies during spawning. The young spend one to two years in nursery lakes before migrating to the sea where they usually spend two or three years before returning to fresh water and spawning.

Next Page - A grizzly bear tries to catch a red salmon leaping Brooks Falls in Katmai National Park and Preserve in Southwestern Alaska. Katmai is the largest sanctuary for grizzly bears in the United States.

Two brown bears *(Ursus arctos)* settle a dispute at the McNeil River State Game Sanctuary in Southcentral Alaska in July. Grizzly bears differ from their brown bear coastal cousins in that they are smaller and inhabit the interior regions of Alaska with less access to plentiful salmon runs.

Above - The shore of Naknek Lake in Katmai National Park and Preserve provides a napping spot for a sow grizzly and her cub on a sunny September afternoon.

Below - A brown bear sow with three yearling cubs is always on the alert for big males that may threaten her offspring in the McNeil River State Game Sanctuary in June. Males sometimes kill the cubs in order to mate with a sow.

Right - Bathed in the warm light of evening, a large grizzly emerges from grass near the Brooks River in Katmai National Park. After eating salmon for three months, bears are fat and in prime condition to hibernate during winter when their metabolism drops dramatically.

Below - A large grizzly bear *(Ursus arctos horribilis)* feeds on a spawned-out red salmon in September along the Brooks River in the Katmai National Park and Preserve.

Left - A black bear *(Ursus americanus)* escorts her young cub over a moss-covered rock at Anan Bay Creek in the Tongass National Forest in Southeast Alaska. Black bears are the smallest and the most common of Alaska's three bear species.

Below - As an early fog begins to clear on a September morning along the Brooks River, two grizzly cubs swim out to join their mother feeding on red salmon.

Left - A mother grizzly bear *(Ursus arctos horribilis)* and her cub prepare to den as the first heavy snow hits Katmai National Park and Preserve in October.

Below - Two grizzly bear cubs romp along the shore of 20-mile long Naknek Lake in Katmai National Park and Preserve while waiting for their mother's return.

Along the Toklat River in Denali National Park wolves attacked, but failed to kill a large bull caribou. The wolves left and hours later a female grizzly bear with three yearling cubs came along. Sensing the caribou was injured, the sow immediately attacked. Although the weakened bull put up a valiant fight, he was no match for the bear. The bear family fed on the caribou for two days.

Grizzly bears *(Ursus arctos horribilis)* can wear many expressions.   This large, scar-faced male at the McNeil River State Game Sanctuary just looked scary.   Note the long lethal claws, which typically grow to four or more inches long.

No one knows for sure why humpback whales *(Megaptera novaeangliae)* breach, but watching 40 tons of whale burst from waters in the Frederick Sound in Southeast Alaska is breathtaking.

Right - Water falls smoothly off the flukes of a diving humpback whale. Most humpbacks spend summers in Alaska in a constant cycle of feeding and resting, then migrate to Hawaii for the winter to breed and raise their calves.

Below - Five humpback whales *(Megaptera novaeangliae)* in Chatham Strait in Southeast Alaska use cooperative bubble-net feeding to catch herring in July. Bubble-net feeding involves surrounding a school of fish with bubbles to confine them and then swimming in to swallow them.

Bottom - A barnacle-encrusted humpback whale makes a magnificent breach in Frederick Sound near Admiralty Island in Southeast Alaska.

Left - A pod of Orca whales *(Orcinus orca)* travels through Icy Strait beneath the St. Elias Mountain range in Southeast Alaska in July. Orcas are also known as killer whales due to their supreme hunting skills for other marine mammals such as seals and whales.

Below - Like wolves, Orca whales travel in pods or family groups. Transient pods can range hundreds of miles in search of fish, birds, seals and other marine mammals to feed on. Resident pods remain in the same area year-round.

Next page - Four large bull caribou *(Rangifer tarandus)* browse amidst fall colors on tundra foliage near Wonder Lake in Denali National Park and Preserve in September.

Left - A large bull caribou in Denali National Park and Preserve has just shed the velvet from his antlers and is ready for the autumn rutting season when mating occurs. Both male and female caribou grow antlers, the only members of the deer family to do so.

Below - Members of the Porcupine caribou herd travel across snow-covered tundra in the central Brooks Range in Northern Alaska in November. There are several major herds of caribou in Alaska, some of which number over half a million. Caribou are always on the move to keep from overgrazing their food supply, which includes moss and lichens.

In September a bull caribou crosses the high tundra in Denali National Park and Preserve as morning light etches a line along Pioneer Ridge leading to Mt. McKinley's North Peak.

A herd of musk oxen *(Ovibos moschatus)* roams free on Nunivak Island in Western Alaska in March. Once hunted to extinction in Alaska, musk oxen were re-introduced from Greenland in 1935 and have rebounded. They now range in scattered herds on the open Arctic tundra of Alaska's northern coast as well.

A large male polar bear *(Ursus maritimus)* prowls the sea in early November. Polar bears rank at the top of the food chain in the animal world, with a diet consisting mainly of seals and an occasional beluga whale or walrus. They also feed on the carcasses of dead bowhead and other whales. They usually give birth to twins in December or January.

Left - Two polar bears decide to play and wrestle in the midst of an arctic blizzard with winds in excess of 50 miles per hour. Polar bears are subject to predation by killer whales, wolves and humans. Male polar bears sometimes will kill cubs, as well.

Right - A large polar bear *(Ursus maritimus)* uses its massive paw to scratch snow from its head after an arctic snowstorm. The bottom of its foot is thickly furred, which muffles sound that prey under the ice would otherwise hear. This is important since ice amplifies noise. Polar bears are only found in the northern hemisphere and inhabit the ice adjacent to five countries: the United States, Canada, Norway, Russia, Greenland.

Below- Early morning light dawns on a polar bear family. The two and a half-year-old twin cubs still need their mother's training and protection, although the cubs will be able to travel a mile or more from their mother to hunt on their own in the spring.

A polar bear closes its eyes to the 50 mph winds and sits out a storm. Normally dwellers on the Arctic pack ice in order to catch seals, polar bears come ashore, but usually stay close to the coast. In addition to meat, they have been known to eat kelp and bird eggs. Near Alaska, they range as far north as 75 degrees and as far south as Nunivak Island. They frequently live 25 to 30 years.